The Imaginative Explorer's Guide to the Park

Eric Braun

BLACK
RABBIT
BOOKS

Hi Jinx is published by Black Rabbit Books
P.O. Box 3263, Mankato, Minnesota, 56002.
www.blackrabbitbooks.com
Copyright © 2021 Black Rabbit Books

Marysa Storm, editor; Michael Sellner, designer;
Omay Ayres, photo researcher

Names: Braun, Eric, 1971- author.
Title: The imaginative explorer's guide to the park /
by Eric Braun.
Description: Mankato : Black Rabbit Books, [2021]
Series: Hi jinx. The imaginative explorer's guide
Includes bibliographical references.
Audience: Ages 8-12 | Audience: Grades 4-6
Summary: "Invites readers to take a fresh, creative
look at the park through playful, conversational text
and fun tips"– Provided by publisher.
Identifiers: LCCN 2019026801 (print) |
LCCN 2019026802 (ebook) | ISBN 9781623103309
(hardcover) | ISBN 9781644664261 (paperback)
ISBN 9781623104245 (adobe pdf)
Subjects: LCSH: Parks–Juvenile literature.
Classification: LCC SB481.3 .B73 2021 (print)
LCC SB481.3 (ebook) | DDC 333.78/3-dc23
LC record available at https://lccn.loc.gov/2019026801
LC ebook record available at https://lccn.loc.gov/2019026802

Printed in the United States. 1/20

Image Credits

Alamy: BNP Design Studio, Cover; iStock: 18–19; denis_pc, 12;
dodo4466, 6–7; olematt, 10–11; Shutterstock: Aleksei Martynov,
4; AnaBoo, 10; benchart, Cover; blambca, 4; BlueRingMedia,
8; chompoo, 4; Cory Thoman, 8; Crystal Eye Studio, 4; Danilo
Sonino, 18–19; Denis Cristo, 12; Dualororua, 2–3; Lorelyn
Medina, 2–3; mark stay, 23; Memo Angeles, 1, 4, 4–5, 5, 8, 14,
14–15, 15, 16–17, 19, 20, 21; mohinimurti, 3, 19, 21;
MSSA, 2–3; Natukach Nataliia, 16–17; NextMars,
Cover, 16, 23; Ollie The Designer, 16;
opicobello, 6–7, 15; Pasko Maksim, 9, 12,
23, 24; pitju, 21; Refluo, 4; Ron Dale, 5, 6, 9,
12, 13, 17, 20; stefanphotozemun, 20;
Tomacco, Cover; Victor Brave, Cover, 16, 23;
Vladislav Kudoyarov, 14–15; your, 11; Every
effort has been made to contact copyright
holders for material reproduced in this book.
Any omissions will be rectified in subsequent
printings if notice is given to the publisher.

Contents

Chapter 1
Get Some Fresh Air

Bored, bored, bored. That's what you are. Bored. You're so bored you had a farting contest with your sister. You won … but at a terrible price. The house now smells horrible! You've been breathing the same air over and over. You better grab your imagination and get outside. There's a park to explore!

More Than Just a Playground

The park is a great place to let your imagination **roam**. It might have a playground or grass area for running and playing. It might also have a creek or a lake. Parks are great places to have fun. Especially if you bring your imagination!

Tip

Be sure to tell an adult where you're going!

Chapter 2
Scavenger Hunts

A park is the perfect place to have a photo **scavenger hunt**. Grab some friends and cameras! Then make a list of things you might find at a park. Come up with at least 10 items. Is it spring or summer? Add dandelions and dog poop to the list. A winter list could have icicles and paw prints in the snow. Then split into teams, set a timer for 20 minutes, and take pictures. Whichever team gets pictures of the most stuff from the list wins.

Tip You could also give awards for the most creative pictures.

Looking for Litter

Scavenger hunts can be a lot of fun. They can also be super helpful. Parks often have litter. Challenge your friends to see who can pick up the most! Whoever throws away the most litter is the winner. And everyone gets to feel good about helping out Earth.

Tip

Someone can pretend to be a TV announcer. They can tell the game's story and talk about the players.

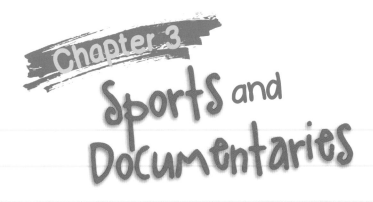

Chapter 3
Sports and Documentaries

Parks often have baseball fields. Head over to the field with some friends. Don't worry about grabbing equipment, though. You don't need any! You're going to play invisible baseball.

Just imagine you have a bat and ball. Pitch the invisible ball. The batter then swings the invisible bat. Crack! The ball flies an incredible distance. The batter runs the bases. A fielder makes a diving catch. What a play! People passing by will be puzzled. Don't worry! That's half the fun. Put on a good show for them.

Out in Nature

Not into sports? That's just fine. You can narrate your own nature documentary instead. Walk around the park and talk about the animals you see. Explain what the animals are doing and why. Pretend you're looking back at a camera. Talk to the camera to share made-up stories and **outrageous** facts. To really make it fun, use an **accent**.

Tip

If you have a smartphone or video camera, film your documentary. Share it with family and friends for a good laugh.

15

Chapter 4
Playing with Portals

Visiting different worlds sounds like it'd take a lot of work. But it's actually super easy. Just bring a bunch of string to the park. Run lines of string between trees to make a rectangle. The rectangle should hang in the air and be upright like a doorway. It's your **portal** to another world. Jump through, and imagine what's on the other side.

Tip

Don't forget to clean up your portal when you're done. You don't want someone to accidentally jump through. Or follow you back!

From a Different World

You can also imagine you're visiting the park from another world! Go to the park in a costume. Pretend you're from a different world or **era**. Act confused by what people at the park are doing. Freak out when you see a squirrel. Small fluffy animals could be evil where you're from!

There's so much to do at the park! All you need is a little imagination.

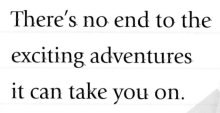

There's no end to the exciting adventures it can take you on.

Chapter 5
Get in on the
Hi Jinx

An imagination can help you have a fun afternoon. It could also help you have a cool job someday. Costume **designers** use their imaginations to make outfits for characters in movies and plays. They might have to dress princesses and knights. Or they might need to make **futuristic** spacesuits. Maybe you'll use your imagination to design costumes someday!

Take It One Step More

1. **Why are parks important parts of neighborhoods?**

2. Imagine you went through a portal to another world. Write a story about your adventure.

3. What other jobs need a good imagination? Make a list. Which do you think you would like best?

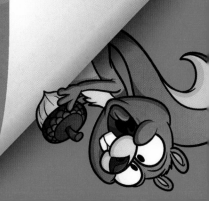

GLOSSARY

accent (AK-sent)—a way of pronouncing words shared by the people of a particular country or region

designer (dih-ZAHY-ner)—a person who plans how something new will look and be made

era (AYR-uh)—a period of time identified by a major event, person, or stage of development

futuristic (fyoo-chuh-RIS-tik)—advanced or very modern

outrageous (out-REY-juhs)—very strange or unusual

portal (PAWR-tl)—a door or gate to a different area

roam (ROHM)—to go from place to place with no fixed purpose or direction

scavenger hunt (SKAV-in-jer HUHNT)— a game in which players try to find specified items within a particular period of time with the help of clues or hints

BOOKS

Devos, Sarah. *I am Never Bored: The Best Ever Craft and Activity Book for Kids: 100 Great Ideas for Kids to Do When There Is Nothing to Do.* Beverly, MA: Quarry Books, an imprint of The Quarto Group, 2018.

Peterson, Megan Cooley. *Pranks to Play Outside.* Humorous Hi Jinx. Mankato, MN: Black Rabbit Books, 2018.

WEBSITES

50 Fun Summer Activities for Kids!
www.unicefkidpower.org/summer-activities-kids/

Crafts & Experiments for Kids
www.pbs.org/parents/activity-finder/ages-all/topics-all/shows-all/types-all

Get Outside!
kids.nationalgeographic.com/explore/nature/get-outside1/

INDEX